EARLY BUDDHISM

EARLY BUDDHISM

BY

T. W. RHYS DAVIDS, LL.D., Ph.D.

PROFESSOR OF COMPARATIVE RELIGION AT OWENS COLLEGE
PROFESSOR OF BUDDHIST LITERATURE, UNIVERSITY COLLEGE, LONDON FELLOW OF THE BRITISH ACADEMY, ETC. ETC.

GYAN

Published by

GYAN

Gyan Publishing House
5, Ansari Road
Daryaganj, New Delhi-110002
Phone: 011-47034999, 9811692060
E-mail: books@gyanbooks.com

Distribution Network
gyanbooks.com
India, USA, Canada, UK, Australia, France

ISBN : 978-81-212-2548-9 (HB)
First Published, 1908

2nd Impression 2021

Printed at: Gyan Press, Delhi.

Early Buddhism
Author: T. W. Rhys Davids

EARLY BUDDHISM

By

T. W. RHYS DAVIDS, LL.D., Ph.D.

PROFESSOR OF COMPARATIVE RELIGION AT OWENS COLLEGE

PROFESSOR OF BUDDHIST LITERATURE, UNIVERSITY COLLEGE, LONDON

FELLOW OF THE BRITISH ACADEMY, ETC., ETC.

LONDON

ARCHIBALD CONSTABLE & CO Ltd

1908

CONTENTS

CONTENTS

EARLY BUDDHISM

CHAPTER I

INTRODUCTORY

The Sâkiya Clan.—The founder of Buddhism was born about 560 B.C. at Kapila-vastu, the principal town in the territory of the Sâkiya clan, situate about one hundred miles nearly due north of Benares.

At that time the Aryan settlers along the lower slopes of the Himâlaya range, and down the valley of the Ganges, had reached a stage of political and social evolution very similar to that reached about the same time in Greece. The country was politically split up into small communities, usually governed under republican institutions, some more aristocratic, some more democratic in character. But in four or five of these republics tyrants had succeeded in enforcing their power over their compatriots, and an irresistible tendency was leading to the absorption of all the small republics in the neighbouring larger kingdoms. Thus the Sâkiya clan was already under the suzerainty of the adjoining kingdom of Kosala.

Kosala.—The exact boundaries of Kosala at that time are not known; but it must have included nearly all of the present United Provinces, together with a large portion of Nepal. Its capital, Sâvatthi, lay in the mountains, in what is now Nepal. Benares, formerly an independent state, was already incorporated under the rising power of this important kingdom, which must have been three hundred miles in length from north to south, and about the same in breadth from west to east—nearly twice the size of England. The supremacy of this warlike clan of mountaineers, and the peace preserved throughout the wide extent of their domain, were the main political factors of the time. And the issue of the struggle, then already in progress, between Kosala and Magadha, its neighbour on the south-east, was about to decide the fate of the great continent of India through the following centuries.

Language of Kosala.—Two points are especially worthy of notice in this connection. In the first place, the language of Kosala, owing to the influence of the court, the army, and the officials stationed throughout its territory, tended to supplant the local dialects. These bore about the same relation to the Vedic speech as Italian does to Latin, and will have differed among themselves about as much as the different dialects of the different counties in England. They were no doubt mutually intelligible. But the particular variety in use in court and official circles became more and more the language in daily use among people of culture or wealth or birth throughout Kosala, a kind of *lingua franca*, the Hindustani of the sixth century B.C. The Buddha, as a native of Kosala, spoke Kosalan. And we can deduce evidence of the condition the language had then reached in its official form from the edicts of Asoka and other early inscriptions; and in its literary form from the Pali, that is the canon, of the sacred books.[1]

The Brahmins.—In the second place, the ruling clan in Kosala was settled to the east and to the north of the portion of India most subject to brahmin influence. The brahmins had not yet, in the districts where Buddhism arose, acquired that supreme authority in social and religious

[1] This question of the language is discussed at length in the present writer's *Buddhist India*; and in Professor Otto Franke's *Pali und Sanskrit*.

questions which they now have in modern India, and which they are represented in Manu and the Epics to have acquired when those books were composed. The Kshatriya clansmen, no doubt, esteemed the brahmins highly; but they esteemed themselves more highly still. They mentioned themselves first, and designated the brahmins as 'of low birth' compared to the Kshatriyas. The position was not quite the same as, but can be better understood by a comparison with, the state of things in Europe during a long period of its history, and even now. The established clergy were, and are, much respected. But in social esteem they rank, not above, but below the nobles. In matters of astrology, the interpretation of dreams and omens, the performance of certain lucky ceremonies, the knowledge of ritual, the people had recourse to brahmins. In matters of ethics, religion, and philosophy they listened rather to the Wanderers.

The Wanderers. — These were wandering teachers, celibates, but not necessarily ascetics, who resembled in many respects the Greek sophists. Like them they differed much in intelligence, earnestness, and honesty. Some are described as 'Eel-wrigglers,' 'Hair-splitters'; and this not without reason, if one may judge fairly from the specimens of their arguments as reported by their adversaries. But there must have been many of a very different character, or the high reputation they enjoyed among all classes of the people would scarcely have been maintained. They held no formal meetings, and made no set speeches; but they used to call on the cultured people in the settlements they visited, and welcomed, in their own lodging places, any one willing to talk of higher matters. So large was the number of such people that the town communities, the clans, and the râjas vied one with another to provide the Wanderers with pavilions, meeting halls, and resting-places where such conversations or discussions could take place.

Some of the Wanderers were women, some were brahmins by birth (not, of course, by profession), but the majority were clansmen. For the three months of the rains they remained in the same spot. The rest of the year they wandered through the land, living on alms, holding their sessions wherever they went. And just as the Strolling Students in pre-Reformation times throughout Central Europe were both a sign of the coming change, and also largely helped to bring it about, so the conditions which made it possible for the Wanderers in northern India to live as they did, were the signs of a general movement in religious and philosophical thought, the foreshadowing of that great uprising which we now call Buddhism.

The Hermits. — Less numerous than the Wanderers, but still an important sign of the times, were the Hermits. Much older in date, the custom of adopting this mode of life has its roots deep in human nature. It is already mentioned in the latest of the Vedic poems, and has maintained its power from that time down to to-day. In one of the earliest of the Buddhist records we have a full statement of the stage it had reached in the Buddha's time, as set forth by a naked ascetic in one of the Dialogues.[1] Dwelling for the most part in the forests, but also in caves in the mountains, the Hermits gave themselves up to renunciation and self-mortification, living on roots and fruits. The professor of self-torture referred to above enumerates twenty-two methods of mortifying the body in respect of food, thirteen in respect of clothing, and five in respect of posture.

As is well known, such ideas are not confined to India. Tennyson, in his monologue of St.

[1] Translated by the present writer in *Dialogues of the Buddha*, vol. i. pp. 226-232.

Simeon Stylites, has given us a powerful analysis of the feelings that lay at the root of similar practices among Christians. But the Indian way of treating the whole conception is more akin to the way Diogenes thought when he lived, like a dog, in his tub-kennel. There is no question of penance for sin, of an appeal to the mercy of an offended deity. It is the boast of superiority advanced by the man able, by strength of will, to keep his body under, and not only to despise comfort, but to welcome pain.

Both in the West and in the East such claims were often gladly admitted. We hear in India of the reverence paid to the man who (to quote the words of a Buddhist poet)—

> 'Bescorched, befrozen, lone in fearsome woods,
> Naked, without a fire, afire within,
> Struggled, in awful silence, toward the goal.'[1]

Simeon, by the acclaim of the populace, became a saint even before he died. Diogenes, and his parallel in India, Mahâvîra the Jain, founded important schools that have left their mark in history. But experience soon shows the other side of the question. In Greece it was the sophists and the philosophers, rather than the

[1] Majjhima, i. 79; quoted Jâtaka, i. 390.

ascetics, who came to be the acknowledged leaders of opinion. In India, it was the newer method of the Wanderers that received, and mainly, as we shall see, through the influence of Buddhist teaching, the higher recognition.

Freedom of Thought.—One remarkable circumstance was that the most perfect freedom, both of thought and of expression, was permitted, not only to Hermits and Wanderers, but to every one else. There had probably never been before, there certainly has seldom been since, any time and place at which such absolute liberty of thought prevailed. This argues a considerable degree of culture, a habit of courtesy and gentleness, among the people; a tolerance all the more noteworthy when we bear in mind the zeal and earnestness of so large a proportion of the community in matters of religion. It is, in fact, a very great mistake to conclude, on the evidence of the priestly law books (which are centuries later), that at this period also the Indians were more superstitious than other folk, more under the thumb of the sacrificial priesthood. All the evidence points the other way. There was, on the contrary, in spite of much naïve speculation and vain sophistry, a real independence of any shackles of authority, a well-marked lay feeling, and a love of humour and irony that was a potent defence.

Economic Conditions.—One reason for the large amount of attention devoted to ethical and philosophical questions was undoubtedly the state of the economic conditions of the period. None of the difficulties that have arisen in modern times were then much felt. The population to be supported were probably barely one-tenth of the number now occupying the same territory. The vast majority of the people were peasant proprietors, living in village communities on their own land, under the supervision of village officers elected by themselves, with power limited by immemorial custom. There was a tithe payable in kind to the government, whether a local republic, or a distant king. Kings sometimes made what was called a grant of a village to some noble, or official, or priest. But this was a grant only of the government dues; and the land still belonged to the peasants, or to the peasant community. There were a few isolated cases of landlords, where a rich man had, by hired labour, made a clearing in the forest. But the number of hired labourers was small. It was considered a disgrace for a free man to let himself out for hire; and though it was difficult for a free-lance to gain admission to an existing village community, there was plenty of land not absorbed in the existing settlements, and open to squatters. The very widely extended inter-state commerce afforded other openings; and the guilds of craftsmen, organised under their own Elders, provided occupation for those who could secure admission to their ranks.

While, therefore, there was but little abject poverty, the number of those who could be considered wealthy from the standpoint of those days (and still more so from our own) was also very limited. We hear of about a score of râjas or mahârâjas, whose income consisted mainly of the land tax supplemented by certain dues and perquisites; of a considerable number of wealthy nobles, and of some wealthy priests; and of about a score of millionaire merchants in the few large towns. There were no great manufacturers and no powerful landlords. The wants of the people were few. And the great mass of them were well-to-do peasantry or handicraftsmen, mostly with land of their own, and troubled neither with poverty nor wealth.

Caste.—There was no caste in India, in those days, in the sense in which that word is now used. There were social grades, technically called

Colours, the boundary lines of which were not always or strictly observed. There were restrictions as to intermarriage, and as to eating together, just as there were then everywhere throughout the world among peoples in a similar stage of culture. Certain trades, especially among the most despised occupations (such as scavengers, leather workers, and butchers), tended to become, a few of them had already become, hereditary. There was a strong feeling on the part of the Aryans of the superiority of their race. But this feeling had not prevented, and did not then prevent, a quite considerable degree of intermarriage. So much, indeed, was this the case, that though there were a considerable number of clansmen, and especially of Kshatriyas and Brahmins, who claimed pure Aryan descent on both sides for seven generations, the number of those whose claims were justified was probably not very large. Mixed up with this question of race there was a good deal of pride of birth, not less than is observed to-day in the West. All these factors were present at the same period among the Aryans in Europe. They were the factors on which the present caste system of India was long afterwards, after the decay of Buddhism, built up. But it was not yet then built up. We have numerous instances in the books which show that the lines were not then at all strictly drawn. The elements, the foundations, of the caste system were there; but the system itself did not, as yet, exist.

CHAPTER II

CONDITION OF RELIGION IN INDIA AT THE TIME OF THE RISE OF BUDDHISM

IT will be necessary, in order to explain the views put forward by the Buddha, to give a summary of the views previously current among the communities in whose territories he taught.

Vedic Beliefs.—And firstly, the views then current were not the views we find enunciated or implied in the thousand and odd Vedic hymns. As, through the centuries, the Aryans had pushed on into the land, their language, through the inevitable laws of the growth, or decay, of a living language, had so altered that they understood the hymns no longer. The hymns were still known only in the schools of the sacrificing priests, and were there split up into texts to be used as charms (*mantras*) in the sacrifice. Beyond the circles of those connected with the schools they were disregarded and unknown. When originally composed in the Panjab, the hymns had included only a portion of the beliefs of the people; and with each generation, with each change of domicile, the gap between the actual beliefs and those recorded in the hymns grew wider and wider.

Death of the Gods.—Such a process is just as inevitable as the change in a living language, or in a living structure. We should never forget in what degree all these their gods were real. They had no objective existence; but they were real enough, for a moment, as ideas in men's minds. At any given time the gods of a nation seem to the onlooker eternal, unchangeable. As a matter of fact they are always slightly changing. No two men, even though brought up in the same surroundings, when they are thinking on the same day of the same god have quite the same mental image. Nor can the proportionate importance of the image be the same to each of them; for that could only be the case if all their other ideas were exactly the same, which, of course, they never are. Just as a man's visible frame, though no change is at any moment perceptible, is never really the same for two consecutive moments, and the result of constant minute variations becomes visible after a lapse of time; so the ideas summed up by the name of a god become changed by the gradual accretion of minute variations. This change, after a lapse of time (it may be generations, it may be centuries), becomes so clear that a new name arises, and gradually, very gradually, ousts the older one. Then the older god is dead. As the Buddhist poet puts it: 'The flowers of the garlands he wore are withered, his robes of majesty have waxed old and faded, he falls from his high estate, and is reborn into a new life.' He lives again, as we might say, in the very result of his former life, in the new god, that is, who under the new name reigns in men's hearts.

The Gods in the Buddha's Time.—We are able to estimate how far this was true in the Buddha's time of the Vedic gods from the statements in two very interesting poems, included by a fortunate chance in the Buddhist canon.[1] These give lists of gods supposed to be friendly to the new teaching. Remarkable as works of art, these lists are of great value as evidence of what the actual deities were whose worshippers the new teaching desired to conciliate. It is most improbable that the unknown poets would have

[1] They are in the Dîgha Nikâya, and have been translated by Gogerly. A new edition of Gogerly's works is now being published in Ceylon.

omitted any deity with a large or influential following. First come the spirits of Mother Earth and of the Great Mountains. Then the Four Great Kings, the lords of the spirits supposed to dwell in all the four quarters of the world, north and south, east and west. These are in the east the Gandharvas, heavenly musicians, supposed to preside over child-birth, and to be helpful in many ways to mortals. In the south are the hungry ghosts, supposed to be full of dire influences, but open to be appeased by the proper means. The west is the special home of the Nâgas, the Siren-serpents, whose worship played so great a part in the folk-lore of the people, and who are so often represented on the monuments. Cobras in the ordinary shape, they were supposed to live, like mermen and mermaids, beneath the waters, in great luxury, especially of gems, or to haunt the giant trees of the forest. They could at will, and often did, adopt the human form; and though terrible if angered, were kindly and mild by nature. To the north, in the mysterious heights of the Himâlayas, were assigned the Yakshas, under their king, Kuvera Vessavaṇa, the god of wealth and prosperity. After these comes in both lists a miscellaneous company—the souls or spirits supposed to animate the moon and the sun (the moon is always mentioned first), the winds, the clouds, the summer heat; then follows a curious assortment of impersonations of various mental qualities; and lastly, the gods who dwell in the highest heavens (that is, are the outcome of the highest speculation), like Brahmā himself, and Paramatta, and Sanang Kumâra.

Without going into any detailed analysis, it is sufficient to state that we find ourselves here, in this description of the religion of the peoples among whom Buddhism arose, face to face with a conception quite different from that recorded in the Vedas, and not even derived from it. Of the hundred or so deities enumerated, barely half-a-dozen are Vedic.

Animism.—The above are the higher gods revered by the people at the time we are considering. The lower forms of animistic delusion popular among them are set forth in another very ancient document entitled 'On Conduct.'[1] It is a list of practices disapproved by the early Buddhists. In the middle of this tract it states that some people are tricksters, droners out of holy words for pay, diviners, exorcists, or earning

[1] In Pali, 'The Sîlas,' a tract translated in my *Dialogues of the Buddha*, vol. i. pp. 3-25.

their living by low arts; and there then follows a list of such low arts. We are told of palmistry, divination of various sorts, auguries drawn from eclipses, prognostications based on dreams, auguries drawn from marks on cloth gnawed by mice, sacrifices to the god of fire, oblations of various kinds to gods, determining lucky sites, laying ghosts, working charms on snakes or beasts or birds, astrology, interpreting signs on the bodies of children, consulting gods by means of a mirror or through a girl possessed; and so on. Some of these undoubtedly refer to practices enjoined in the priestly books. Others cannot be traced there. And the whole list is proof, if such were needed, that then, in the valley of the Ganges, as elsewhere, all kinds of the animism that had preceded the book religion had also survived in sufficient degree to continue to afford, to those who would condescend to take advantage of it, opportunity for gain.

The Soul Theory.—Further than that the evidence does not, I think, take us. It is a matter of degree. There was, one would be inclined to think, an almost universal and unquestioned belief in the existence, round and about, of an infinite number of non-human beings. These the people took as a matter of course, just as they took the existence of souls inside their own bodies as a matter of course. It was by these souls, within them and without, that they explained to themselves the mysteries of death and trance and dreams, of motion and of life. Handed down from an immemorial antiquity, this hypothesis or theory of souls was current at that time in India, just as it has been current before and since among civilised and uncivilised races throughout the world.

Endless were the applications of this theory, the methods of explanation for which it was used. To enumerate and explain them all (for the applications of it often need a good deal of explanation) would fill volumes. A man falls in a faint, and then comes to again. It is clear that it is his soul that has gone away for a time, and then come back to him. The majestic sun passing in his daily path across the firmament, so resplendent a centre of life and heat and motion, must be alive. It is animated as men are by a soul, only that its soul is more glorious, more powerful, than theirs. The giant monarch of the forest, stretching its weird arms through the dusk, contains a soul, a Nâga, a tree-fairy, whose thought and action explain all the mysteries of the tree. And so on, through the long list of those objects that appeared to man's senses as fearsome, bounteous, mysterious, inspiring awe.

The Forms of Worship.—All these souls were supposed to have human passions, human nature, even human form. They were amenable, like humans, to flattery and presents; and could be compelled by charms to do, or to refrain from doing, what the workers of the charm desired. The Vedic sacrifices, as performed by brahmins at this period, were almost exclusively of this magical character. For these there were no temples. One of the main sources of emolument to the priests was the building, accompanied by the use of many charms, of a new altar for each sacrifice. The altar was put up on private ground, and the sacrifice was a private ceremonial designed to secure personal advantages to the person at whose cost the sacrifice was carried out. There were no images of the gods. These sacrifices being long and very costly were also therefore rare, and could only be carried out by the wealthy. That was perhaps an additional reason why the mass of the people, at the period and in the districts we are considering, followed other gods. Of their cults we unfortunately know very little, and that only as yet from incidental references in the Buddhist books. We are told of chetiyas or shrines, and their names and approximate situations are known. Some are supposed to have been burial mounds, and others sacred trees. But we know as yet next to nothing as to what was done there. No pre-Buddhistic shrine in India has, so far, been excavated; and the incidental references to them in the books have not been collected and studied. So also we hear of *Samajjas*, clan meetings on sacred heights, with dances sacred and secular, and other accompaniments of what in modern times we might expect to find at a fair. But the references to these meetings presuppose in their readers a knowledge of all that went on, and of what it really meant. And that is precisely what we should like to know.

Speculation.—On the other hand we have fairly detailed and intelligible accounts of what, as compared with the local cults, may be called the higher speculation. In records older than the Buddhist we see the monistic mysticism, which reached its highest expression in the theosophic poetry of the Upanishads, gradually taking shape. And in the earliest Buddhist books we not only have the names of various sects or groups, either of Wanderers or Hermits, but elaborate classifications of a large number of the theories held by them. The names are suggestive: The Unfettered, the Followers of the Shaveling, the Men of braided hair (these are brahmin hermits), the Bearers of the triple staff, the Friends, the Worshippers of the god (we are not told which), the Men of pure livelihood, and so on. The theories are given, in the first of the Dialogues, in a list that is too long to reproduce. There are thirty-six different views as to the state, after the death of the body it inhabited, of the soul; and one theory that the soul dies when the body dies. Curiously enough the theory of the transmigration of souls is not referred to; and the theory of the absorption of the individual soul into the supreme soul is not mentioned. There are a number of divergent views as to whether all the gods, or only some, or only one should be considered eternal; and as to how far the world and individual souls are eternal. And there are discussions as to ethics, and as to the various means of salvation in this life.

Summary of Beliefs.—We have, then, in India in the valley of the Ganges at the time when Buddhism arose, a maze of interacting ideas which may be divided, for clearness in exposition, under the following heads:—

Firstly, the very wide and varied group of ideas about souls supposed to dwell within the bodies of men and animals, and to animate moving objects in nature (trees and plants, rivers, planets, and so on). These may be summed under the convenient modern term of *Animism*.

Secondly, we have later and more advanced ideas about the souls supposed to animate the greater phenomena of nature. These may be summed up under the convenient modern term of *Polytheism*.

Thirdly, we have the still later idea of a unity lying behind all these phenomena, both of the first and of the second class, the hypothesis of a one first cause on which the whole universe in its varied forms depends, in which it lives and moves, and which is the only reality. This may be summed up in the convenient modern term of *Monism*.

Fourthly, we have the opposite view. In this the first cause has either not been reached in thought, or has been considered and deliberately rejected: but otherwise the whole soul-theory has been retained and amplified, and the hypothesis of the eternity of matter is held at the same time. This may be summed up under the convenient modern name of *Dualism*.

These modern Western terms, though useful for classification, never exactly fit the ancient Eastern thought. And we must never forget that the clear-cut distinctions we now use were then perceptible to only quite a few of the clearest thinkers. Most of the people held a strange jumble of many of the notions current around them. The enumeration here made is merely intended to show that, when Buddhism arose, the country was seething, very much as the Western world was at the same period, with a multitude of more or less opposing theories on all sorts of questions, ethical, philosophical, and religious. There was much superstition, no doubt, and no little sophistry. But owing partly to the easy economic conditions of those times, partly also to the mutual courtesy and intellectual alertness of the people, there was a very large proportion of them who were earnestly occupied in more or less successful attempts to solve the highest problems of thought and conduct.

CHAPTER III

LIFE OF THE BUDDHA

Edifying Poetry.—If an Eastern scholar desired to ascertain the facts about the life of Christ he would not have recourse to such works as Klopstock's *Messiah* or Milton's *Paradise Regained.* They do not even purport to be historical. Such value as they have is due to the literary skill with which they recast a story derived from earlier documents; and perhaps also to the part they play as *Tendenzschriften*, as supporting a certain trend of opinion. The historical inquirer would go to the original documents, he would ignore the later poetry.

It is unfortunately precisely such later books of edifying poetry that have been the source of modern popular notions about the life of the Buddha. Sir Edwin Arnold's well-known poem, *The Light of Asia*, is an eloquent expression in English verse (based on the *Lalita Vistara*) of Buddhist beliefs at the time when, centuries after the time of the Buddha, the Sanskrit poem was composed. Any one who wishes to know the truth, so far as it can now be ascertained, about the actual events of the Buddha's life will obviously ignore these productions, however edifying, of literary imagination. He will go to the earliest documents.

No Buddhist Gospel.—The first discovery he would make is that there is no book in the Buddhist Canon exactly corresponding to a gospel. The nearest approach to one is the *Mahâparinibbâna-Suttanta*, the Book of the Great Decease, describing the last journey of the Buddha, and his death.[1] Besides this we have two considerable episodes: one describing the time before his attainment, under the Wisdom Tree, of Nirvana, and the other describing the events that immediately followed.[2] Apart from these consecutive narratives there are accounts more or less circumstantial, in many of the Dialogues, of various episodes in Gotama's career. Some of the ancient ballads and poems also relate to such episodes; and there are other incidental references elsewhere in the literature.

The Buddha not a King's Son.—From these

[1] Translated in my *Dialogues of the Buddha*, vol. ii.

[2] Majjhima, i. 163-175, and Vinaya, i. 1-44.

notices, scanty as they are, it is quite possible to piece together a very clear idea as to the main events in the life of the founder of Buddhism. His father is, in one passage,[1] called a *râja*. But râja is a courtesy title used of any member of the recognised clans; and the texts, always punctilious in the use of titles, never use this word of a king, who is invariably styled *mahārāja*. The family is lauded, in half-a-dozen passages, as well connected, and of high repute; but not once as royal. We may be sure, from the context, that had the future Buddha's father been really a king the fact would, in this connection, have been clearly stated. As used of the clansmen generally the title *râja*, though really of not much more weight than our modern 'esquire,' was more polite, as the word connoted a position of hereditary importance in the clan, and perhaps even a temporary official post, of an honorary character, such as consul or archon. In any case this was the simple basis on which the latter legends of royalty were built up.

The Family and Clan.—His father's name, Suddhodana, Pure Rice, is suggestive of the occupation followed by the clan. It occupied a small territory, not exceeding about nine hundred square miles in

[1] Dîgha, ii. 7. Compare Buddhavangsa, xxvi. 13.

extent, partly on the lower slopes of the Himâlayas, partly on the plains below. There the clansmen had their rice-fields watered by the unfailing streams fed from the heights behind. All the year round they had in full view the glorious snow peaks of the great mountains, and the breezes from the north brought down to them the breath of the glaciers. When I was in the lower part of the Sâkiya territory, just over the Nepal frontier, in January 1900, the climate was cool and pleasant. No doubt in the summer it would be desirable to escape into the hills. And we are told[1] that, in his youth, the future Buddha had three homes, one for the winter, one for the summer, and one for the rainy season; and that he was clad, not in coarse cloth, but in fine muslin of Benares.

The Lumbini Garden.—The boy was named Siddhattha, that is 'desire accomplished,' and the meaning of the name may have given rise to the story, found only in the later legends, that he was born after the hope of a son had almost passed away. The family name was Gotama. By that he was usually addressed in after life by non-Buddhists, and it is the name we shall use in this sketch.

[1] Anguttara, i. 45. Compare Digha, ii. 21

His father's home was at Kapilavastu, in the plains, the capital town of the clan, where their Mote Hall was situate. But he was born, as a very ancient ballad tells us, at Lumbini.

This was a pleasaunce half way between Kapilavastu and the chief town of the Koliyans, neighbours and relatives of the Sâkiyas. The later explanation, that his mother was then on her way to be confined at her mother's house, sounds very probable. The exact spot assigned by tradition to this event has lately been rediscovered. A pillar, erected on the site by Asoka, in the middle of the third century B.C., states that 'Here the Exalted One was born.'

The ballad just referred to, 'The Nâlaka Sutta,'[1] is most interesting. The poem describes how an old man of wisdom, Asita by name, seeing the angels rejoice, asks them why they are glad. They say:—

> 'The Wisdom Child, that jewel so precious,
> That cannot be matched,
> Has been born in Lumbini, in the Sâkiya land,
> For weal and for joy in the world of men.'

So the old sage goes there, and sees the babe, and prophesies:—

[1] Translated by Professor Fausböll in *Sacred Books of the East*, vol. x. p. 124.

'The topmost height of insight will he reach, this child, he will see that which is most pure, and will set rolling the chariot wheel of righteousness, he who is full of compassion for the multitude. Far will his religion spread.'

The going forth.—Gotama was married; and had one son whose name was Râhula. When he (the father, that is) was twenty-nine years of age, he left his home and became a *religieux* 'to seek after what was right.'[1] Thus early in the career of the future teacher do we find the ethical trend of his mind and action emphasised. Many writers in East and West have suggested reasons for this momentous step; and some things plausible, some beautiful, have been said. Our authoritative texts have but two short utterances on this point, both put into the mouth of the Buddha himself. The first is as follows:—[2]

'An ordinary unscholared man, though himself subject to old age, not escaped beyond its power, when he beholds another man old is hurt, ashamed, disgusted, overlooking the while his own condition. Thinking that that would be unsuitable to me the infatuation of a youth in his youth departed utterly from me.'

[1] Dîgha, ii. 151.

[2] Anguttara, i. 146.

Then identical words are used of health and life. The other text says:—

'Before the days of my enlightenment, when I was still only a Bodhisat, though myself subject to rebirth, old age, disease, and death, to sorrow and to evil, I sought after things subject also to them. Then methought: Why should I act thus? Let me, when subject to these things, seeing the danger therein, seek rather after that which is not subject thereto, even the supreme bliss and security of Nirvana.'[1]

The gist of all the later poetry is found in these simple but pregnant words; and the oldest poem we have keeps very closely to the spirit of these equally ancient texts. It is the following ballad which, as it is short, can be quoted. Even in a bald prose version it will give a taste of the spirit of those far-off days.

THE GOING FORTH

1. I will praise going forth as the far-seeing One did, the Wanderer's life, such as when he had thought the matter out he deliberately chose.

2. 'Full of hindrances is this household life, the haunt of passion. Free as the air is the homeless state.' Thus he considered, and went forth.

[1] Majjhima, i. 163.

3. When he had gone forth he gave up wrong-doing in action, and evil speech he left behind; pure did he make his mode of livelihood.

4. To the king's town the Buddha[1] went, to Giribbaja in Magadha. Full of outward signs of worth, he was collecting alms for food.

5. Him saw Bimbisâra standing on the upper terrace of his palace. On seeing that he had those signs, thus did he speak:—

6. 'Hearken to this man, Sirs, handsome is he, great and pure; guarded in conduct, he looks not more than a fathom's length before him.

7. 'With downcast eye and self-possessed is he, surely of no mean birth. Let the king's messengers hasten and find out: Where is the mendicant going?'

8. Thus sent, the messengers hurried after him, and asked themselves: 'Where is the Bhikshu going, where does he mean to stay?

9. 'Going on his round for alms regularly from house to house, guarded as to the door (of his senses), well restrained, quickly has he filled up his bowl, he the while calm and self-possessed.

10. 'His round for alms accomplished, the Sage has

[1] This expression is suggestive. In our sense of the word, Gotama was not yet a Buddha. To the mind of the poet Buddha meant merely 'awakened' (its literal meaning). The corresponding word in Christian technical usage would be 'converted.' And the mind of the converted man is awakened, but to different conceptions. It is very doubtful whether in old texts the word Buddha ever means anything more than 'awakened.'

gone out from the town. He has gained the mountain Paṇḍava. There is it that he means to stay.'

11. No sooner had they seen him stop than the messengers in their turn stopped. One messenger alone returned, and to the king made speech :—

12. 'On the eastern slope of Mount Paṇḍava, that Bhikshu, O King, has taken his seat, like a tiger-king, like a lion in his mountain cave.'

13. When he heard his servant's word the warrior, in all haste, went forth in his state chariot to the mountain Paṇḍava.

14. Where the carriage-road ended, there alighting from his car, on foot the prince went on till he came near; and then he took his seat.

15. On sitting down the king, with courteous words, exchanged with him the greetings of a friend. Then he spake thus :—

16. 'Young art thou and of tender years, a lad in his first youth, fine is thy colour like a high-born noble's.

17. 'As the glory of the vanguard of the army, at the head of a band of heroes I would give thee wealth. Do thou accept this, and tell me thy lineage now that I ask it.'

18. 'Hard by Himâlaya's slopes, O King, there is a land of wealth and power, the dwellers therein are of the Kosalas;

19. 'Descendants of the Sun by race, Sâkiyas they are by birth. 'Tis from that clan I have gone forth, longing no more for sensual delights.

20. 'Seeing the danger in them, looking on going

forth as bliss, I shall go on in the struggle, for in that my mind delights.'

His Teachers.—Gotama had now become a Wanderer. Whether before or after his interview with the King of Magadha we do not know, he attached himself as a disciple first to Âlâra Kâlâma, and afterwards to Uddaka son of Râma. Centuries later certain writers pretend to know their doctrines. In the old texts we are only told that each of these teachers held out as an ideal a particular stage of mystic ecstasy (whether mental only, or the result of self-induced hypnotism, or partly one, partly the other, is not stated).[1] And two mystic utterances of Uddaka's have also been preserved.[2] Beyond this we know nothing of what, or even where, they taught. Whatever it was, Gotama so quickly mastered it that they each asked him to become co-teacher of their band of disciples. But these offers he refused, as he had refused Bimbisâra's, and went out into the forest round Gayâ to struggle on by himself to the light.

The Struggle.—We have several accounts of this struggle given in nearly identical words.[3]

[1] Majjhima, i. 163-166.

[2] Saṃyutta, iv. 83, and Pâsâdika Suttanta in the Dîgha.

[3] Majjhima, i. 17-24 ; 114-118 ; 167 ; 240-250.

No attempt is made to give a consecutive or chronological relation of what happened in the six years during which it lasted. The various severe penances that Gotama inflicted on himself are described at length; and various thoughts that occurred to him, subjects that he discussed with himself, are enumerated. At the end of the penances, when he was worn to a skeleton, and indeed at the point of death, he resolves that this is not the right path to enlightenment, and begins again to take nourishment. Thereupon, we are suddenly told:[1] 'Then those five mendicants [of whom no previous mention had been made] forsook him, and went away, on the ground that he had given up the struggle, and gone back to a life of abundance.'

To this time we have probably to refer the ballad[2] in which Mâra, the Evil One, is represented as tempting him to give up the quest.

The Nirvana.—Then comes the reaction, the victory. This is uniformly described as a mental state of exaltation, bliss, insight, altruism. The different Suttas emphasise different phases, different facets as it were, of this condition. But they

[1] Majjhima, i. 247.

[2] Translated by Fausböll in *Sacred Books of the East*, vol. x. pp. 69-71.

regard it as one and the same upheaval of the whole mental and moral nature,—will, emotion, and intellect being equally concerned. Thus one Sutta (the Mahâ-saccaka) lays stress on the four Raptures, and the three forms of Knowledge; another (the Dvedhâ-vitakka) on the certainty, the absence of doubt; another (the Bhaya-bherava) on the conquest over fear and agitation; another (the Ariya-pariyesanâ) on the bliss and security of the Nirvana to which he then attained.

In the first of these Suttas the recital ends:—

'When this knowledge, this insight, had arisen within me, my heart was set free from the intoxication of lusts, set free from the intoxication of becomings, set free from the intoxication of ignorance. In me, thus emancipated, there arose the certainty of that emancipation. And I came to know: "Rebirth is at an end. The higher life has been fulfilled. What had to be done has been accomplished. After this present life there will be no beyond." This last insight did I attain to in the last watch of the night. Ignorance was beaten down, insight arose, darkness was destroyed, the light came, inasmuch as I was there strenuous, aglow, master of myself.'

There is nothing miraculous in it all, nothing

supernatural. Supranormal it undoubtedly is. But recent researches in psychology, such as are summed up, for instance, in James's *Varieties of Religious Experience*, show that phenomena of a similar kind, though not quite the same, are well authenticated in the lives of men of deep religious experience. And no one of all the experiences described in these accounts is, in the canonical books, confined to the Buddha. Each of them is related, in other passages, of one or other of the men and women who afterwards adopted the new teaching and fell under its influence. These conditions are constituent parts of the state of mind called Arahatship. They all recur in the standard description, repeated in so many of the Dialogues, of the manner in which Arahatship is reached.[1] And the sum of them is, in this connection, called Nirvana,[2] one of the many epithets of Arahatship.[3] In the opinion of the early Buddhists their Buddha was an Arahat; but in his case there was no limit at all to the depth and intensity of his insight, or to the grace and perfection of those powers and characteristics he shared with other Arahats. The distinction

[1] Translated in full in my *Dialogues of the Buddha*, vol. i. pp. 79-93.

[2] Majjhima, i. 167.

[3] *Ibid.* 173.

between Arahat and Buddha became the main factor in the subsequent history of the community.[1] In the early passages here referred to as descriptive of this crisis, there is no mention either of Buddha or of Buddhahood.

After Gotama had thus attained Nirvana (if we use the expression of the text), or attained to Buddhahood (if we use the expression which soon became of use in the community), he remained for four times seven days 'enjoying the bliss of emancipation.'[2] The records give us several episodes revealing the thoughts that passed through his mind during that time. He reiterates the twelve Nidânas, the links in the chain of dependent origination, and then gives utterance to three stanzas, to the effect that when an Arahat, in moments of intense insight, sees into the real nature of things, how they all have a cause and how the causes tend to pass away, then his doubts fade away, and he remains steadfast, putting to rout the armies of the Evil One, just as the sun fills the dark spaces of the sky with light.[3]

[1] See *Later Buddhism*, published in this series of small manuals, and my note on Sambodhi in the *Dialogues of the Buddha*, vol. i. p. 190.

[2] Vinaya, i. 1-4.

[3] Vinaya, i. 2, translated by Oldenberg in *Vinaya Texts*, i. 78.

The phrase in this last verse is probably the origin of the legend in another authority[1] that the Evil One then came to him and tempted him, now that he had won the victory, to pass away at once. But he refuses to do so 'till the wonder-working truth shall have been spread abroad, well proclaimed among men.'

Then a haughty brahmin, who relied for salvation on the utterance of the mystic syllable Om, comes by and asks Gotama what makes a man a brahmin. He is answered that it is the putting away of evil, the living of a life of purity, the conquest of haughtiness and greed.

The next episode gives us a stanza explaining the basis of the bliss that he is said to have felt:—

> 'Happy the solitude of him who is full of joy,
> Who has learnt the Truth, who has seen the Truth.
> Happy he who in this world has no ill-will,
> Self-restrained to all beings that have life.
> Happy is freedom from lusts, the getting right away from them,
> The highest bliss is freedom from the pride of the thought "I am."'

The Hesitation.—At the end of this period of bliss follows a period of hesitation, in which Gotama doubts, whether, after all, it will be of

[1] Dîgha, ii. 112, translated by the present writer in *Dialogues of the Buddha*, vol. ii.

any use to proclaim to a world sunk in darkness a doctrine not only so difficult to grasp, but so repugnant to the ordinary mind. We may estimate the importance attached by the early church to this matter by the fact that Brahmâ himself, the highest of the gods, is introduced as coming on the scene to urge that there will still be some who will have eyes to see. Then the Buddha, 'out of compassion for sentient beings,' determines to preach the word. A similar experience is related in identical words [1] of other early Indian teachers, the previous Buddhas. And this overpowering sense of utter apartness, aloofness, is an experience that falls sooner or later to the lot of all great leaders of thought.

The First Discourse.—When this resolve to preach the word had become clear in the Buddha's mind, he is said to have walked to Benares, about one hundred miles to the northwest, to tell his former companions, who were then in a wood near that city, of the discovery he had made. He did so in a discourse entitled, the 'Foundation of the Kingdom of Righteousness,' in which his new views of life were summarised in a way they would understand. This summary has been preserved to us in two places

[1] Dîgha, ii. 37.

in the canon, and will be translated and explained in the next chapter. Buddhist poets have been moved to descriptions of the scene, descriptions remarkable for much subtle beauty. Buddhist sovereigns have lavishly decorated with architecture and sculpture the spot memorable for what they considered so memorable an event. Had a Greek been passing at the time he would have scarcely stooped to notice the few barbarians seated under the trees, talking quietly in earnest tones; and would have scarcely realised that one of them was giving utterance to ideas that would move the world.

The Buddha had no easy task in trying to persuade the five to give up their belief in penance. Only one of them, a Koṇḍañña by birth, was at first convinced—to be known for the rest of his life as 'the Koṇḍañña who understood.' But in the course of a few days all of them had given way, and become disciples. Gotama then advanced a step further, and discoursed to them on the absence of any sign of soul in the constituent elements of a human being. An outline of this discourse has also been preserved in several parts of the scriptures;[1] and

[1] Saṃyutta, iii. 66, and iv. 34; Majjhima, i. 135 and 300; Vinaya, i. 14.

when they had been convinced of this the record states, 'Then there were six Arahats in the world.' From being merely disciples, followers, they had become Arahats.

The Sending Forth of the Disciples.—Then ensued what has many points of analogy with a modern revival, but it must have been of a strangely dignified and intellectual sort. Residents in the neighbouring townships came to listen to the new teacher. The number of adherents, laymen, and laywomen, Bhikshus and Arahats, increased until the record states, 'Then there were sixty-one Arahats in the world.' At that time Gotama said to them that he and they 'were free from snares, whether human or divine. Let them, therefore, go forth as wanderers for the sake of the many, for the welfare of the many, out of compassion for the world, for the good and the weal and the gain of gods and men. No two were to go together. They were to make known the teaching, lovely in its origin, lovely in its progress, lovely in its consummation, both in the spirit and in the letter; to explain the higher life in all its fullness and in all its purity.'[1] As for himself he was going back to Uruvela with that purpose in view.

[1] Saṃyutta, i. 105, reproduced in Vinaya, i. 21.

According to our authorities, the success of this first mission was very great. It is but natural to suppose that it loomed somewhat larger in the eyes of the early Buddhists than the facts actually warrant. But it has been shown above how very favourable were the conditions for a new movement of this kind; and, either then or soon afterwards, we know that the new teaching did become a power in the land. From this time forth Gotama, who from being a Wanderer had become a Hermit, now became a Wanderer again. Those of his followers who 'went forth' became members of the Order he founded, and were also Wanderers, that is, they abjured all penance and self-mortification (unless their vow of celibacy be reckoned as such). Both he and they spent nine months of each year in wandering from village to village, and making the new doctrine known, as they went, to such as cared to hear. They held no public meetings, gave no set discourses: the propaganda was by way of conversation only.

Gotama's Daily Life.—The manner in which Gotama spent each day is somewhat as follows. He rose quite early, about 5 A.M. If he were to stay at the place where he had slept he would remain alone till it was time to go on his round for alms to the neighbouring village. If he were moving from one place to another, a walk of from eight or ten miles would occupy the time. He was often invited for the morning meal, the principal meal of the day, to some particular house. If not he took his bowl, and went from house to house, collecting enough for the meal, which was always over before sun-turn. When he was an invited guest he would, after the meal, 'give thanks,' as the phrase ran, in the form of a talk on some one or other of the more elementary points of religion. When he carried his meal back to his lodging-place this thanksgiving would take the form of an exhortation or dialogue with the disciples on one of the deeper matters of the faith. The heat of the day was given up to repose or meditation. As the afternoon drew in, either the journey to the next stage was resumed, or if the stay in the same place was to be prolonged, an informal reception was held under the trees. The folk from the neighbouring villages would come in, bringing presents of flowers; and one of the visitors, either a layman or a recluse of some other Order, would ask questions or start a discussion, the rest listening as they sat round on the grass under the trees. By sundown the assembly was dismissed. Then Gotama, should he feel so inclined, was wont to take his bath;

after which he would talk with the disciples, perhaps far into the night.

The current Methods of Publishing.—In so steady and warm a climate such an open-air life was not only possible but agreeable; and in the absence of any books, libraries, or newspapers, such a method of instruction and of propaganda was probably the best available. Any one who had anything to say could not sit in his study, write a book, and publish it to the world. He had to gather round him a number of adherents, followers, disciples (call them what you will), persuade them to understand, and learn by heart, his doctrines; and then send them forth into the world. *They* were his books. His personal influence over them, their adaptability, earnestness, and intelligence were factors quite as important for his success as the intrinsic value and fitness for the times of his teaching itself. It was a method of publication that had been used before, and was being used in Gotama's time by others besides himself. The necessity of adopting this method was also one of the main practical reasons for the establishment of an Order. Without the Order the new teaching could neither have been propagated among the people then, nor have been preserved for future generations.

For forty-five years after his attainment of Nirvana, Gotama went up and down through the plains of Northern India and the neighbouring highlands of Nepal. During this period he had ample time both to work out his system very fully, and to instruct the disciples in its details. They are really very few and simple. Such difficulty as European scholars find is concerned with the translation into Western language of certain of the technical terms that were used. There is none of the elaborate minuteness characteristic of the priestly books of ritual exegesis. Most of the earlier Buddhist technical terms must have been chosen and defined within the teacher's life-time; and it is highly probable that the actual words of the short paragraphs in which most of the essential points—the Three Signs, the Four Truths, the Five Hindrances, the Eightfold Path, the constituents of Arahatship, and so on—were also settled by him.

Gotama died, full of years and held in high esteem by the clansmen, when he was eighty years old, at Kusinârâ, a site not yet identified, but probably in Nepal. After the cremation, carried out by the clansmen of the Mallas, in whose territory the town lay, the ashes are said to have been divided into eight portions. Of these six were given to the six clans in the neighbourhood, one being the Sâkiyas, one was given to the King of Magadha, and one to a brahmin in Veṭhadîpa near by. Stûpas or cairns are said to have been put up over all eight; but only one of these has as yet been rediscovered. This is the one put up by the Sâkiyas in the new Kapilavastu, built after the destruction of the older town a few years before the Buddha's death, by Viḍûḍubha, King of Kosala.

CHAPTER IV

THE ARYAN PATH

THE summary of the main features of his system of beliefs which Gotama is said, in our earliest authorities, to have put before his five friends at Benares, gives us what those authorities held to be most important in his teaching. We may possibly go even further. It is not very probable, after the long and careful course of instruction they had received from him, that the early disciples can have misunderstood him on such a point. There are distinct traces in our earliest documents of a development of thought in the views of his followers regarding the personality of their master, in their Buddhology. No such traces have yet been found of development in fundamental doctrine. The balance of probability is therefore in favour of the tradition having preserved the actual views of Gotama himself; and very possibly the expressions he used. But even if we adopt the more difficult hypothesis, and suppose that the tradition embodies the views of the early disciples, and that they invented these utterances, put forward by them as the first discourse of their Master,—even then we have in these words the oldest and most authoritative statement of Buddhist doctrine that we possess.

The Word Aryan.—In the text, preserved in two separate places in the Canon,[1] the Path pointed out is called the Aryan path, the Truths enumerated are called the Aryan truths. The word Aryan is ambiguous. Already in the Vedas it means both 'of Aryan race' and 'gentle, noble, kindly.' Some etymologists give different derivations for the different meanings. It is more probable that the second meaning is derived from the first, just as our word gentle meant originally of gentle birth. By the time of the rise of Buddhism, the secondary meaning had become so fixed in the connotation of the word that it conveyed all the senses of belonging to the Aryan race, gentle and noble. In some passages the stress is laid upon the point of race, in others on the ethical, in others on the æsthetic side. But all three were present together to the minds of speakers and hearers alike. In the text we

[1] Saṃyutta, v. 420, and Vinaya, i. 10.

are now discussing, all three would be applicable, and were probably meant to be implied. I have rendered the word 'noble'; and that translation can easily be defended. But I am inclined to think that at least one idea hinted at by the use of this epithet was, that the new system then promulgated was considered worthy of, suitable for, the free clansmen, for the men of Aryan race. The Buddhist commentators, writing long afterwards, when the word had quite lost its racial sense, always interpret it as meaning 'worthy of, suitable for Arahats.' And there are several passages in the old texts in which *Ariya* and Arahat are used as synonymous terms.[1] This is only one of many instances of a new, and as the speakers thought, a better, deeper meaning being put into older words, and may, therefore, have been intended by Gotama in this case also.

One other remark by way of introduction is necessary. The words we have are a condensed summary of a talk that lasted over some days. Whoever chose the words, they are very carefully chosen. To translate them without using words with a Christian bias or modern ideas is not easy, as so many excellent English words are

[1] For instance Majjhima, i. 280, and my wife's note at Duka Paṭṭhâna, i. 366.

thus shut out. Every word is important, and it is a great pity that, in popular works on Buddhism, the expressions have been usually further condensed (which they will not bear), or so altered as to misrepresent the meaning. The full text is as follows:—

'*There are two extremes which he who has gone forth*[1] *ought not to follow—habitual devotion on the one hand to the passions, to the pleasures of sensual things, a low and pagan way (of seeking satisfaction), ignoble, unprofitable, fit only for the worldly-minded; and habitual devotion, on the other hand, to self-mortification, which is painful, ignoble, unprofitable. There is a Middle Path discovered by the Tathâgata*[2]*—a path which opens the eyes, and bestows understanding, which leads to peace, to insight, to the higher wisdom, to Nirvana. Verily! it is this Aryan Eightfold Path; that is to say Right Views, Right Aspirations, Right Speech, Right Conduct, Right mode of livelihood, Right Effort, Right Mindfulness, and Right Rapture.*

'*Now this is the Noble Truth as to suffering.*

[1] See above p. 31.

[2] That is by the Arahat; the title the Buddha always uses of himself. He does not call himself the Buddha; and his followers never address him as such.

Birth is attended with pain, decay is painful, disease is painful, death is painful. Union with the unpleasant is painful, painful is separation from the pleasant; and any craving unsatisfied, that, too, is painful. In brief, the five aggregates of clinging (that is, the conditions of individuality) are painful.

'Now this is the noble Truth as to the origin of suffering. Verily! it is the craving thirst that causes the renewal of becomings, that is accompanied by sensual delights, and seeks satisfaction, now here now there—that is to say, the craving for the gratification of the senses, or the craving for a future life, or the craving for prosperity.

'Now this is the Noble Truth as to the passing away of pain. Verily! it is the passing away so that no passion remains, the giving up, the getting rid of, the emancipation from, the harbouring no longer of this craving thirst.

'Now this is the Noble Truth as to the way that leads to the passing away of pain. Verily! it is this Aryan Eightfold Path, that is to say, Right Views, Right Aspirations, Right Speech, conduct, and mode of livelihood, Right Effort, Right Mindfulness, and Right Rapture.'

A few words follow as to the threefold way in

which the speaker claimed to have grasped each of these Four Truths. That is all. There is not a word about God or the soul, not a word about the Buddha or Buddhism. It seems simple, almost jejune; so thin and weak that one wonders how it can have formed the foundation for a system so mighty in its historical results. But the simple words are pregnant with meaning. Their implications were clear enough to the hearers to whom they were addressed. They were not intended, however, to answer the questionings of a twentieth-century European student, and are liable now to be misunderstood. Fortunately each word, each clause, each idea in the discourse is repeated, commented on, enlarged upon, almost *ad nauseam*, in the Suttas.[1] A short comment in the light of those explanations, though it can only be a repetition of what I have often said before, is necessary to bring out the meaning that was meant.

The End of Pain.—The passing away of pain or suffering is said to depend on an emancipation. And the Buddha is elsewhere (Vinaya i. 239) made to declare: 'Just as the great ocean has one taste only, the taste of salt, just so have this

[1] See, for instance, Dîgha, ii. 305 to 307, and 311 to 313; Majjhima, iii. 231; Saṃyutta, v. 8; Paṭisambhidâ, i. 37-42.

doctrine and discipline but one flavour only, the flavour of emancipation.' And again: 'When a brother has, by himself, known and realised, and continues to abide, here in this visible world, in that emancipation of mind, in that emancipation of heart which is Arahatship—that is a condition higher still, and sweeter still, for the sake of which the brethren lead the religious life under me.' [1]

The emancipation is found in a habit of mind, in the being free from a specified sort of craving that is said to be the origin of certain specified sorts of pain. In some European books this is completely spoiled by being represented as the doctrine that existence is misery, and that desire is to be suppressed. Nothing of the kind is said in the text. The description of suffering or pain is, in fact, a string of truisms quite plain and undisputable until the last clause. That clause declares that the five *Upâdâna Skandhas*, the five groups of bodily and mental qualities that make up an individual, involve pain.

Pain and Individuality.—One can express that in more modern language by saying that the conditions that make an individual are precisely the conditions that also give rise to pain. No sooner

[1] Mahāli Suttanta; translated in Rhys Davids, *Dialogues of the Buddha*, vol. i. p. 201. Compare p. 204.

has an individual arisen, become separate, than disease and decay begin to act upon it. Individuality involves limitation, limitation involves ignorance, ignorance ends in sorrow. All the sorts and sources of pain here specified—birth, decay, death, union with the pleasant, separation from the pleasant, unsatisfied longings—are each simply a result of individuality. This is a deeper generalisation than that which said: 'A man is born to trouble as the sparks fly upward.' But it is put forward as a mere statement of fact. And the previous history of religious belief in India would tend to show that emphasis was laid on the fact, not as an explanation of the origin of evil, but rather as a protest against the then current pessimistic idea that salvation could not be reached on earth, and must therefore be sought for in rebirth in heaven. For if the argument were admitted, it would follow that even in heaven the individual would still be subject to sorrow; and by admitting this the five ascetics, to whom the words were addressed, would have to admit also all that followed.

Craving.—The threefold division of craving at the end of the second truth might be rendered: 'The lust of the flesh, the lust of life, and the love of this present world.' The two last are said elsewhere to be directed against two sets of thinkers, called the Eternalists and the Annihilationists, who held respectively the everlasting-life heresy, and the let-us-eat-and-drink-for-to-morrow-we-die heresy.[1] This may be so. But in any case the division of craving would have appealed to the five hearers as correct.

Impermanence.—The details of the Path include several terms whose meaning and implication are by no means apparent at first sight. Right views, for instance, mean mainly right views as to the Four Truths and the Three Signs. Of the latter, one is identical, or nearly so, with the First Truth. The others are Impermanence, and non-soul (the absence of a soul)—both declared to be 'signs' of every individual, whether god, animal, or man. Of these two, again, the Impermanence has become an Indian rather than a Buddhist idea; and we are familiar enough with it also in the West. There is no Being, there is only a Becoming. The state of every individual is unstable, temporary, sure to pass away. Even in things we find, in each individual, Form and other Material qualities. In living organisms there is a continually ascending series of Mental qualities also. It is the

[1] See *Iti-vuttaka*, p. 44; Saṃyutta, iii. 57.

union of these that makes the individual. Every person, or thing, or god is therefore a putting together, a compound. And in each individual, without any exception, the relation of its component parts is ever changing, is never the same for two consecutive moments. It follows that no sooner has separateness, individuality, begun, than dissolution, disintegration, also begins. There can be no individuality without a putting together: there can be no putting together without a becoming: there can be no becoming without a becoming different: and there can be no becoming different without a dissolution, a passing away, which sooner or later will inevitably be complete.

Herakleitos, who was a generation or two later than the Buddha, had very similar ideas;[1] and similar ideas are found in post-Buddhistic Indian works.[2] But in neither case are they worked out in the same uncompromising way. Both in Europe, and in all Indian thought except the Buddhist, souls, and the gods who are made in imitation of souls, are considered as exceptions. To these spirits is attributed a Being without Becoming, an individuality without

[1] Burnet, *Early Greek Philosophy*, p. 149.
[2] Katha Up., 2.10; Bhag. Gîtâ 2.14; 9.33.

change, a beginning without an end. To hold any such view would, according to the doctrine of the Noble (or Aryan) Path, be erroneous, and the error would block the way against the very entrance on the Path.

So important is this position in Buddhism that it is put in the forefront of Buddhist expositions of Buddhism. The Buddha himself is stated in the books to have devoted to it the very first discourse he addressed to the first converts.[1] The first in the collection of the Dialogues of Gotama discusses and completely, categorically, and systematically rejects all the current theories about 'souls.' Later books follow these precedents. Thus the Kathâ Vatthu, the latest book included in the canon, discusses points of disagreement that had arisen in the community. It places this question of 'soul' at the head of all the points it deals with, and devotes to it an amount of space quite overshadowing all the rest.[2] So also in the earliest Buddhist book later than the canon—the very interesting and suggestive series of conversations between the Greek King Menander and the Buddhist teacher

[1] The Anatta-lakkhaṇa Sutta (Vinaya, i. 13 = Saṃyutta, iii. 66 and iv. 34), translated in *Vinaya Texts*, vol. i. pp. 100-102.

[2] See my article on *Buddhist Schools of Thought* in the *J.R.A.S.* for 1892.

Nâgasena. It is precisely this question of the 'soul' that the unknown author takes up first, describing how Nâgasena convinces the king that there is no such thing as the 'soul' in the ordinary sense. And he returns to the subject again and again.[1]

Right Desires.—After Right Views come Right Aspirations. It is evil desires, low ideals, useless cravings, idle excitements that are to be suppressed by the cultivation of the opposite—of right desires, lofty aspirations. In one of the Dialogues[2] instances are given—the desire for emancipation from sensuality, aspirations towards the attainment of love to others, the wish not to injure any living thing, the desire for the eradication of wrong, and for the promotion of right, dispositions in one's own heart; and so on. This portion of the Path is indeed quite simple; and would require no commentary were it not for the still constantly repeated blunder that Buddhism teaches the suppression of all desire.

Right Effort.—Of the remaining stages of the Path it is only necessary to mention two. The

[1] *Questions of King Milinda*, translated by Rhys Davids (Oxford, 1890-1894), vol. i. pp. 40, 41, 85-87; vol. ii. pp. 21-25, 86-89.

[2] Majjhima, iii. 251. Compare Saṃyutta, v. 8.

one is Right Effort, a constant intellectual alertness is required. This is not only insisted upon elsewhere in countless passages, but of the three cardinal sins in Buddhism (*râga, dosa, moha*) the last and worst is stupidity or dullness, the others being sensuality and ill-will. Right Effort is closely connected with the seventh stage, Right Mindfulness. Two of the Dialogues are devoted to this subject, and it is constantly referred to elsewhere.[1] The disciple, whatsoever he does—whether going forth or coming back, standing or walking, speaking or silent, eating or drinking,—is to keep clearly in mind all that it means, the temporary character of the act, its ethical significance, and, above all, that behind the act there is no actor (goer, seer, eater, speaker) that is an eternally persistent unity. It is the Buddhist analogue to the Christian precept: 'Whether therefore ye eat or drink, or whatsoever ye do, do all to the glory of God.'

Love.—Under the head of Right Conduct the two most important points are Love and Joy. Love is in Pali *Mettâ*, and the Mettâ Sutta[2] (no

[1] Dîgha, ii. 290-315; Majjhima, i. 55 fol. Compare Rhys Davids, *Dialogues of the Buddha*, p. 81.

[2] No. 8 in the Sutta Nipâta (p. 26 of Fausböll's edition). It is translated by Fausböll in vol. x. of the *S.B.E.* and by Rhys Davids, *Buddhism*, p. 109.

doubt with reference to the Right Mindfulness just described) says :—

'*As a mother, even at the risk of her own life, protects her son, her only son, so let him cultivate love without measure towards all beings. Let him cultivate towards the whole world—above, below, around—a heart of love unstinted, unmixed with the sense of differing or opposing interests. Let a man maintain this mindfulness all the while he is awake, whether he be standing, walking, sitting, or lying down. This state of heart is the best in the world.*'

Often elsewhere four such states are described, the *Brahma Vihâra* or Sublime Conditions. They are Love, Sorrow at the sorrows of others, Joy in the joys of others, and Equanimity as regards one's own joys and sorrows.[1] Each of these feelings was to be deliberately practised, beginning with a single object and gradually increasing till the whole world was suffused with the feeling.

'*Our mind shall not waver. No evil speech will we utter. Tender and compassionate will we abide, loving in heart, void of malice within. And we will be ever suffusing such an one with the rays of our loving thought. And with that*

[1] Dîgha, ii. 186, 187.

feeling as a basis we will ever be suffusing the whole world with thought of love, far-reaching, grown great, beyond measure, void of anger or ill-will.[1]

The relative importance of Love, as compared with other habits, is thus described:—

'*All the means that can be used as bases for doing right are not worth the sixteenth part of the emancipation of heart through Love. That takes all those up into itself, outshining them in radiance and glory. Just as whatsoever stars there be, their radiance avails not the sixteenth part of the radiance of the moon. That takes all those up into itself, outshining them in radiance and glory—just as in the last month of the rains, at harvest time, the sun, mounting up on high into the clear and cloudless sky, overwhelms all darkness in the realms of space, and shines forth in radiance and glory—just as in the night, when the dawn is breaking, the Morning Star shines out in radiance and glory—just so all the means that can be used as helps towards doing right avail not the sixteenth part of the emancipation of heart through Love.*'[2]

Joy.—The intense bliss, pervading the whole being, which follows on the assurance of salvation

[1] Majjhima, i. 129. [2] *Itivuttaka*, pp. 19-21.

won, is independent of the dogmas or beliefs of those who have felt the disenchantment, passed through the struggle, and won the victory. We have undoubted and most interesting examples among the adherents of the most antagonistic forms of Christian belief. And Moslem Sufis and Buddhist Arahats have had the same experience. There are preserved in the canon two collections of the Songs of the Elders, ascribed respectively to one hundred and seven men and seventy-three women who became Arahats in the life-time of the Buddha. They are, with a very few exceptions, pæans of joy and victory. They have, unfortunately, not been translated as yet into English; but the spirit they breathe is shown in the following prose passage.[1] After pointing out that the Hindrances (Nîvaraṇâ)—sensuality, ill-will, torpor of mind or body, worry, and wavering—affect a man like debt, disease, imprisonment, slavery, and anxiety—it goes on:—

'*When these five Hindrances have been put away within him, he looks upon himself as freed from debt, rid of disease, out of jail, a free man, and secure. And gladness springs up within him on his realising that, and joy arises to him thus gladdened, and so rejoicing all his frame*

[1] Taken from my *Dialogues of the Buddha*, vol. i. p. 84.

becomes at ease, and being thus at ease he is pervaded with a sense of peace, and in that peace his heart is stayed.'

There is a string of verses in the Dhammapada on this state of bliss, the Right Rapture, the last stage of the Path. The following is one of them:—

'It is in very bliss we dwell, we who hate not those who hate us;
Among men full of hate, we continue void of hate.
It is in very bliss we dwell, we in health among the ailing;
Among men weary and sick, we continue well.
It is in very bliss we dwell, free from care among the careworn;
Among men full of worries, we continue calm.
It is in very bliss we dwell, we who have no hindrances;
We will become feeders on joy, like the gods in their shining splendour!' [1]

Another verse from the same anthology says:—

'When the wise man by earnestness hath driven
Vanity far away, the terraced heights

[1] Dhammapada, verses 197-200.

Of wisdom doth he climb, and, free from care,
Looks down on the vain world, the careworn crowd—
As he who stands upon a mountain top
Can watch, serene himself, the toilers in the plains.'[1]

[1] Dhammapada, verse 28.

CHAPTER V

THE LIONS IN THE PATH

THOUGH the texts are full of assurance of the possibility of happiness here, in this world, without waiting for a better, they are not blind to the opposite side of the question, and recognise, frankly and fully, the obstacles and dangers. As usual, in the absence of books, these were arranged, for the convenience of memory, into classes. The most dangerous are the five Hindrances (see above p. 63), the ten Bonds, and the four Intoxications. The Bonds are:—

1. Delusions about the soul (Sakkâya-ditthi).
2. Doubt (Vicikicchâ).
3. Dependence on works (Sîlabbata-parâmâsa).
4. Sensuality (Kâma).
5. Ill-will (Paṭigha).
6. Desire for rebirth on earth (Rûpa-râga).
7. Desire for rebirth in heaven (Arûpa-râga).
8. Pride (Mâno).

9. Self-righteousness (Uddhacca).
10. Ignorance (Avijjâ).

These words are all perfectly simple, except six and seven, which are explained below. The curious thing is that these evil dispositions are supposed to be conquered in order—so that, for instance, to conquer delusions about the soul is the very entrance on the Path, and to conquer Ignorance (the direst foe, the worst enemy of the human race) is only possible at the end of it. I am not prepared to say there is not some reason in this, especially when we consider the frequent instances, in the texts, of individuals, in moments of spiritual exaltation or insight, breaking three, or four, or five of the Bonds at a bound. To have broken the first three Bonds is what we should call conversion, what they call 'the entrance into the stream.' And as the doctrine of Final Assurance is part of early Buddhism, there can then be no permanent relapse. Sooner or later, in this or another birth, final salvation is assured.

The Intoxications.—The intoxications were originally three—the mental infatuation arising from sensual pleasures, from the pride of life, and from ignorance respectively. Then there was added a fourth. This addition must have been made very early in the progress of the new movement; and it is of remarkable interest from the point of view of the history of human thought. It was the infatuation arising from speculation—speculation as to uncertainties, ultimate causes, questions of no moment for the practical conduct of life. The stigma thus attached to this sort of speculation was the most formidable attack that had been made so far, in the history of the world, on theology and metaphysics. The rival theories purported to explain the origin and end of all things, to be able to give a clear and absolute decision as to the finiteness or infinity of the world, as to the eternity of the soul, and of those bigger souls, the gods. Buddhism declares that everything has a cause, the cause (or causes) included; that there is nothing permanent; and that it is not only a sufficient, it is the only true, method to argue from one cause back to the next, and so on, without any hope, or even desire, to explain the ultimate cause of all things. The most famous of all Buddhist stanzas, found engraved on ten thousand votive gifts to Buddhist shrines in India, put, in the Canon, into the mouth of the fifth of the Arahats, and quoted as authoritative in the works of all but the very latest of the various schools of Buddhist thought, tells us:—

> '*Of all the phenomena sprung from a cause*
> *The Buddha the cause hath told,*
> *And he tells too how each shall come to its end,*
> *Such alone is the word of the Sage.*'[1]

The Indeterminates.—This position seemed to many of Gotama's contemporaries to be a confession of failure. And it was a failure from the point of view of those to whom precisely such questions seemed of the utmost importance. But Gotama was perfectly firm. He refused not only to answer, but even to discuss such points. They were of course being constantly raised. His answer was a list of Indeterminates, questions barred.

1, 2. Whether the world is eternal or not.

3, 4. Whether the world is infinite or not.

5, 6. Whether the soul is the same as the body, or different from it.

7-10. Whether a man exists in any way, or not, after death.[2]

There were others; but these are the ones most frequently mentioned.

[1] Vinaya, i. 40. Compare Îsâ Upanishad, 14. E. Hardy in the *Netti*, p. xxiii.

[2] For references, see my discussion of the Indeterminates in *Dialogues of the Buddha*, vol. i. p. 186 fol.

'*On such points brahmins and recluses stick,*
Wrangling on them they violently discuss;
Poor folk! they see but one side of the shield.'

Such expressions as the following are several times found in the Dialogues:—

The jungle, the desert, the puppet-show, the writhing, the entanglement of such speculations is accompanied by sorrow, wrangling, resentment, the fever of excitement. It conduces neither to detachment of heart, nor to freedom from lusts, nor to tranquillity, nor to peace, nor to wisdom, nor to the insight of the higher stages of the path, nor to Nirvâna.'[1]

We find here two propositions: Do not let us discuss things on which we have not good evidence. Do not let us discuss things which are no use, no good, but the contrary, for us. Whether right or wrong, both propositions seem to me quite intelligible. Subtle arguments have, however, been brought forward to show that, behind this deliberate silence of Gotama, there lay, after all, a covert and esotéric belief, not communicated to his disciples, in a future life and other points of his opponents' creed. That, to me, is not intelligible.

How possible Gotama's position is can be seen

[1] Majjhima, i. 431, 485.

from Frederic Harrison's description of a similar view held now in Europe:—

'When men of high moral and intellectual power assure us that they find rest, unity, and fruit in . . . conceptions about themselves, their own natures, the external world, its origin, construction, and maintenance, the future state of what they conceive to be some part of, or the essence of, themselves, . . . far be it from us to dispute the value and reality of this knowledge. . . . If we do not adopt them, it is not because we believe them to be false, but because they fail to interest us. We can get no practical good out of them.'[1]

Or compare this, from a very different school. Professor James says:—

'Is the world one or many? fated or free? material or spiritual?—here are notions either of which may or may not hold good of the world; and disputes over such notions are unending. The pragmatic method in such cases is to try to interpret each notion by tracing its respective practical consequences.'[2]

The Buddha was neither Comtist nor Pragmatist. But these extracts may show how un-

1 *Philosophy of Common Sense* (London, 1907), p. 40.
2 *Pragmatism* (London, 1907), p. 45.

necessary it is to try to read between the lines of very distinct passages to the contrary in order to find in them the metaphysical sweetmeats dear to so many hearts. In any case, it is clear that to the early Buddhists the habit of theosophic speculation was by no means the least dangerous of the Lions in the Path.

To have realised the Truths, and traversed the Path; to have broken the Bonds, put an end to the Intoxications, got rid of the Hindrances, mastered the craving for metaphysical speculation was to have attained the ideal, the Fruit, as it is called, of Arahatship. One might fill columns with the praises, many of them among the most beautiful passages in Pali poetry and prose, lavished on this condition of mind, the state of the man made perfect according to the Buddhist faith. Many are the pet names, the poetic epithets, bestowed upon it, each of them—for they are not synonyms—emphasising one or other phase of this many-sided conception—the harbour of refuge, the cool cave, the island amidst the floods, the place of bliss, emancipation, liberation, safety, the supreme, the transcendental, the uncreated, the tranquil, the home of ease, the calm, the end of suffering, the medicine for all evil, the unshaken, the ambrosia, the immaterial, the imperishable, the abiding, the further shore, the unending, the bliss of effort, the supreme joy, the ineffable, the detachment, the holy city, and many others. Perhaps the most frequent in the Buddhist texts is Arahatship, 'the state of him who is worthy'; and the one exclusively used in Europe is Nirvana, the 'dying out,' that is, the dying out in the heart of the fell fire of the three cardinal sins—sensuality, ill-will, and stupidity.[1]

The choice of this term by European writers, a choice made long before any of the Buddhist canonical texts had been published or translated, has had a most unfortunate result. Those writers did not share, could not be expected to share, the exuberant optimism of the early Buddhists. Themselves giving up this world as hopeless, and looking for salvation in the next, they naturally thought the Buddhists must do the same; and in the absence of any authentic scriptures to correct the mistake, they interpreted Nirvana, in terms of their own belief, as a state to be reached after death. As such they supposed the 'dying out' must mean the dying out of a 'soul'; and endless were the discussions as to whether this meant eternal trance, or absolute annihilation, of the soul. It is now thirty years since I first put

[1] Saṃyutta, iv. 251, 261.

forward the right interpretation.[1] But outside the ranks of Pali scholars the old blunder is still often repeated. It should be added that the belief in salvation in this world, in this life, was really implicit, though never clearly or openly expressed, in pre-Buddhistic thought. And it appealed so strongly to Indian sympathies that from the time of the rise of Buddhism down to the present day it has been adopted as a part of general Indian belief, and *Jîvanmukti*, salvation during this life, has become a commonplace in the religious language of India.

[1] In the first edition of my manual *Buddhism*, published by the Society for Promoting Christian Knowledge in 1877.

CHAPTER VI

ADOPTED DOCTRINES—KARMA

Transmigration.—The above are the essential doctrines of the original Buddhism. They are at the same time the distinctive doctrines: that is to say, the doctrines that distinguish it from all previous teaching in India. But the Buddha, while rejecting the sacrifices and the ritualistic magic of the brahmin schools, the animistic superstitions of the people, and the pantheistic speculations of the poets of the pre-Buddhistic Upanishads, still retained the belief in transmigration. This belief—the transmigration of the soul, after the death of the body, into other bodies, either of men, beasts or gods—is part of the animistic creed, and is so widely found throughout the world that it was probably universal. In India it had already, before the rise of Buddhism, been raised into an ethical conception by the associated doctrine of *Karma*, according to which a man's social position in life and his physical advantages, or the reverse, were the result of his actions in a previous birth.[1] The doctrine thus afforded an explanation, quite complete to those who could believe it, of the apparent anomalies and wrongs in the distribution here of happiness or woe. A man, for instance, is blind. This is owing to his lust of the eye in a previous birth. But he has also unusual powers of hearing. This is because he loved, in a previous birth, to listen to the preaching of the law. The explanation could always be exact, for it was scarcely more than a repetition of the point to be explained. It fits the facts because it is derived from them. And it cannot be disproved, for it lies in a sphere beyond the reach of human inquiry.

The Bridge.—It was because it thus provided a moral cause that it was retained in Buddhism. But as the Buddha did not acknowledge a soul, the link of connection between one life and the next had to be found somewhere else. The Buddha found it (as Plato also found it[2]) in the influence

[1] Compare *S'at. Br.*, translated by Eggeling, i. 267, with *Chândogya Up.*, 5-10, *Brihad Âr. Up.*, vi. 2-15, and *Kaushîtakî Up.*, p. 146 (ed. Cowell).

[2] *Phædo*, 69 fol. The idea is there also put forward in connection with a belief in transmigration.

exercised upon one life by a desire felt in the previous life. When two thinkers of such eminence (probably the two greatest ethical thinkers of antiquity) have arrived independently at this strange conclusion, have agreed in ascribing to cravings felt in this life so great, and to us so inconceivable, a power over the future life, we may well hesitate before we condemn the idea as intrinsically absurd. And we may take note of the important fact that, given similar conditions, similar stages in the development of religious belief, men's thoughts, even in spite of the most unquestioned individual originality, tend, though they may never produce exactly the same results, to work in similar ways, however strange.

Modes of Karma.—In India, before Buddhism, conflicting and contradictory views prevailed as to the precise mode of action of *Karma,* and we find this confusion reflected in Buddhist theory. The prevailing views are tacked on, as it were, to the essential doctrines of Buddhism, without being thoroughly assimilated to them, or logically incorporated with them. Thus in the story of the good layman Citta, it is an aspiration expressed on the death-bed,[1] in a dialogue on the subject it is a thought dwelt on during life,[2] in

[1] Saṃyutta, iv. 302.
[2] Majjhima, iii. 99 fol.

the numerous stories in the Peta and Vimâna Vatthus it is usually some isolated act; in the discussions in the Dhamma Sangaṇi it is some mental disposition, which is the *Karma* (Doing or Action) in the one life determining the position of the individual in the next. These are really conflicting propositions. They are only alike in the fact that in each case a moral cause is given for the position in which the individual finds himself now, and the moral cause is his own act.

The New Body.—In the popular belief, followed also in the brahmin theology, the bridge between the two lives was a minute and subtle entity, called the soul, which left the one body at death, (usually through a hole at the top of the head), and entered into the new body. The new body happened to be there, ready, with no soul in it. The soul did not make the body. In the Buddhist adaptation of this theory, no soul, no consciousness, no memory, goes over from one body to the other. It is the grasping, the craving, still existing at the death of the one body that causes the new set of skandhas, that is, the new body with its mental tendencies and capacities, to arise. How this takes place is nowhere explained.

East and West.—The Indian theory of Karma

has been worked out with many points of great beauty and ethical value. And the Buddhist adaptation of it, avoiding some of the difficulties common to it and to the allied European theories of fate, providence, and predestination, tries to explain the weight of the universe in its action on the individual; the heavy hand of the immeasurable past we cannot escape, the close connection between all forms of life, and the mysteries of inherited character. The European theories lay the stress upon the future, the Indian on the past. A sufferer believing in the soul, and in fate, or providence, can say: 'This was pre-ordained, I must submit,' and he can try to rectify the balance of justice by assuming a remedy, for which he has no evidence, in a more satisfactory world beyond the grave. If he believes in Karma he will think: 'This is my own fault.' And he can try to rectify the balance of justice by assuming an identity, for which he has no evidence, between himself and some one else in the past.

The Indian theories lay stress upon a law, the European theories upon the action of a sovereign will. And it is very suggestive that the mistake in the Platonic and Buddhist view is precisely the very same mistake against which Buddhism, in the case of the soul-theory, entered so strong a protest. Early Buddhism recognised all the qualities, feelings, etc., included under the term 'soul'; but it said that the mistake lay in postulating an eternal unity instead of a changing plurality. In the case of Karma, it was Buddhism itself that put a unity where a plurality should be; it represented the action of past lives on present ones—which is a profound truth—as the action of a past life on a present one, in a manner not supported by the facts of experience.

How can we explain this difference of method? Is it not because in Karma the Buddhists found, at one and the same time, a moral cause, a reign of law, and an escape from the endless waves of the dark ocean of transmigration? And the fact underlying the Indian theory of Karma is acknowledged to be very real. The history of an individual does not begin with his birth. He has been countless æons in the making. And he cannot sever himself from the past; no, not for a moment. The tiny snowdrop droops its fairy head just so much, and no more, because it is balanced by the universe. It is a snowdrop, not an oak, because it is the outcome of the Karma of an endless series of past existences; and because it did not begin to be when the flower opened, or when the mother-plant first peeped above the ground, or first met the embraces of the sun, or at any point in time which you or I can fix. A great American writer says:—

'It was a poetic attempt to lift this mountain of Fate, to reconcile with liberty this despotism of Race, which led the Hindoos to say "Fate is nothing but the deeds committed in a prior state of existence." I find a coincidence in the extremes of Eastern and Western speculation in the daring statement of the German philosopher Schelling: "There is in every man a certain feeling that he has been what he is from all eternity."'

We may put a new and a deeper meaning into the words of the poet:—

'. . . Our deeds follow us from afar,
And what we have been makes us what we are.' [1]

[1] No one has yet attempted to write a history of the growth in India of the various forms of the Karma theory. Professor Hopkins has a suggestive paper on it in the *Journal of the Royal Asiatic Society* for 1906. On the Buddhist side the reader may consult Rhys Davids's *Buddhism* (S.P.C.K.), 21st ed., pp. 93-106, and Dahlke's *Aufsätze zum Verständnis des Buddhismus* (Berlin, 1903), i. 92-106, and ii. 1-11.

CHAPTER VII

ADOPTED DOCTRINES (*continued*): COSMOGONY. WHEEL OF LIFE

The Kalpas and World-Systems.—Another Indian idea had a great influence on the Buddha's view of life. Just as the doctrine of Karma brought every Indian thinker face to face with immeasurable periods of time, in the past more especially, but also in the future; so the views as to the world brought him face to face with immeasurable realms in space. In the oldest Buddhist texts it is taken for granted that there are ten thousand world-systems, in which expression ten thousand merely means an incalculably large number. They are arranged throughout space in groups of three; and are subject to a continual process of disintegration and evolution. The time occupied by one such process, that is from the commencement of the dissolution to the completion of the restoration, was called a Great

Æon, or *Mahâ Kalpa.* And each Great Æon was divided into four Incalculables, *Asankheyyas.* In later books the details are worked out with a wealth of numbers running into millions. In the older texts we find only the general scheme still quite vague in its immensity. The scheme has not been traced in pre-Buddhistic writings; but, for reasons too long to specify here, I have no doubt it was, in its essential points, older than the rise of Buddhism.

I venture to think that these ideas of the immensity of time and space, of the insignificance, compared with the universe, of our own world-system; of the essential unity between man and all animals (and even plants); of the immense periods of the disintegration and reconstruction of each world-system; of the fact that all things, the whole universe, is in a process of becoming, must have contributed very largely to the conclusions reached as to the immense peril and evil of transmigration, as to the complete hopelessness of looking for any salvation in any other world, as to the essential necessity of a system of mental and moral training, self-mastery, becoming, that would ensure security and happiness here and now. This conclusion will probably be considered inevitable by those who recollect how large a part the then current ideas of cosmogony played in the scholastic theology of Europe; and how great was the change brought about generally in European thought by the new ideas as to the position of our world, and as to the evolution of man. The details of the Buddhist scheme, as worked out in later times by the commentators, are all quite wrong. The general scheme itself, as held in the Buddha's time, is not accurate. But it was so very much nearer to the actual facts than the theory held, in the sixth century B.C., anywhere else in the world, that it would certainly lead to historical error were we to omit to attach to it a very great importance in our estimate of the probable reasons for the growth of early Buddhism.

The Wheel of Life.—There is found in several places in the Canon the following formula:—

1. On account of Ignorance, the Sankhâras.
2. On account of the Sankhâras, Consciousness.
3. On account of Consciousness, Name and Form.
4. On account of Name and Form, the six Provinces (of the six senses).
5. On account of the six Provinces, Contact.
6. On account of Contact, Sensation.
7. On account of Sensation, Craving.

8. On account of Craving, Attachment.
9. On account of Attachment, Becoming.
10. On account of Becoming, Birth.
11, 12. On account of Birth, old age, and death, grief, lamentation, suffering, dejection, and despair.

This formula, called the Paticca-Samuppâda (origination through dependence), is repeated, and certain explanations of the terms used are given. But there is nowhere any explanation, intelligible to modern ideas, as to why each link in the chain causes the next, or even as to the exact meaning of the words. The consequence is that no two scholars agree as to its interpretation. I have discussed it in my *American Lectures*, but am not particularly enamoured of my explanation. It seems to me to be an attempt (and, of course, an unsuccessful one, for the notion is wrong) to describe the way in which the Karma in one life makes an individual in the next. If that be so, clauses 1 and 2 refer to the previous, clauses 3-9 to the present, and clauses 10 to 12 to the future birth.

Now Professor Jacobi has shown that in Yoga and Sânkhya writings some centuries later than the Buddha there are found expressions somewhat similar to these, though not arranged in a chain, and referring to successions of psychological experience in a single birth. The technical terms used are indeed not the same, and it sometimes requires no little subtlety to harmonise them. But there is enough similarity to show that similar ideas as to the succession of psychological states were current in non-Buddhist schools of thought at the time when those writings were composed. The Buddhist formula stands outside the main tenets of the system, like mistletoe on an oak, and could be cut out without modifying the system in any appreciable degree. The theory of the action of Karma in producing a new individual was certainly borrowed. It would seem very likely that this chain, designed to explain the process, was also either borrowed, or adapted, from some previous chain.

Ecstasy.—Another point of Buddhist teaching adopted from previous belief was the practice of ecstatic meditation. In the very earliest times of the most remote animism we find the belief that a person, rapt from all sense of the outside world, possessed by a spirit, acquired from that state a degree of sanctity, was supposed to have a degree of insight, denied to ordinary mortals. In India from the Soma frenzy in the Vedas, through the mystic reveries of the Upanishads, and the hypnotic trances of the ancient Yoga, allied beliefs and practices had never lost their importance and their charm. It is clear from the Dialogues,[1] and other of the most ancient Buddhist records, that the belief was in full force when Buddhism arose, and that the practice was followed by the Buddha's teachers. It was quite impossible for him to ignore the question; and the practice was admitted as a part of the training of the Buddhist Bhikshu. But it was not the highest or the most important part, and might be omitted altogether. The states of Rapture are called Conditions of Bliss, and are regarded as useful for the help they give towards the removal of the mental obstacles to the attainment of Arahatship.[2] Of the thirty-seven constituent parts of the Buddha's teaching they enter into one group of four. To seek for Arahatship in the practice of ecstasy alone is considered a deadly heresy.[3] So these practices are both pleasant in themselves, and useful as one of the means to the end proposed. But they are not the end, and the end can be reached without them. The most ancient form these exercises

[1] For instance, Majjhima, i. 163-166.

[2] Anguttara, iii. 119.

[3] Dîgha, i. 38.

took is recorded in the often-recurring paragraphs translated in my *Dialogues of the Buddha* (i. 84-92). More modern, and much more elaborate, forms are given in the *Yogâvacara's Manual of Indian Mysticism as Practised by Buddhists*, edited by me from a unique MS. for the Pali Text Society in 1896. In the introduction to this last work the various phases of the question are discussed at length.

There are other points on which earlier thought and practice had prepared the way for Buddhism. And as we know approximately both the date of the Buddha's activity, and that of the earliest Buddhist texts, these points of resemblance will be of the greatest value when a history of philosophy in India comes to be written. But the ones here mentioned are perhaps those of most importance. And we may conclude in the words of Professor Huxley, at the end of his exposition of early Buddhism :—[1]

'A system which knows no God in the Western sense, which denies a soul to man; which counts the belief in immortality a blunder, and the hope of it a sin; which refuses any efficacy to prayer or sacrifices; which bids men look to nothing but their own efforts for salvation; which, in its

[1] Romanes Lecture, London, 1893, p. 21.

original purity, knew nothing of vows of obedience and never sought the aid of the secular arm; yet spread over a considerable moiety of the old world with marvellous rapidity, and is still, with whatever base admixture of foreign superstitions, the dominant creed of a large fraction of mankind.'

SELECTED WORKS ON EARLY BUDDHISM

TRANSLATIONS

Rules of the Order

Vinaya Texts, by Rhys Davids and Oldenberg. Oxford, 1881-5.

Doctrine

Buddhist Suttas, by Rhys Davids. Oxford, 1881.
Dialogues of the Buddha, by Rhys Davids, vol i. Oxford, 1899.
Buddhism in Translations, by H. C. Warren. Cambridge, Massachusetts, 1896.
Die Reden des Gotamo Buddho, by K. E. Neumann. Leipzig, 1896-1908.

Abhidhamma

Buddhist Psychology, by Mrs. Rhys Davids. London, 1900.

Tales and Poetry

The Jâtaka, edited by E. B. Cowell. 6 vols. Cambridge, 1895-1908.
Buddhist Birth Stories, by Rhys Davids. London, 1880.
Dhammapada and Sutta Nipâta, by Max Müller and V. Fausböll. Oxford, 1881.
Udâna, by Major-General Strong. London, 1902.
Lieder der Mönche und Nonnen, by K. E. Neumann. Berlin, 1899.
Der Wahrheitspfad, von K. E. Neumann. Leipzig, 1893.

Selected Works, *continued*—

MANUALS AND ESSAYS

OLDENBERG.—*Buddha.* 5th ed. Berlin, 1906. English translation of 1st ed. by W. Hoey. London, 1882.

RHYS DAVIDS.—*Buddhism.* 21st ed. London, 1907. Translated into Dutch, Amsterdam, 1879; into German, Leipzig, 1899.

RHYS DAVIDS.—*American Lectures.* 2nd ed. London and New York, 1906.

DAHLKE.—*Aufsätze zum Verständnis des Buddhismus.* Berlin, 1903. English by J. M'Kechnie. London, 1908.

NARASU.—*The Essence of Buddhism.* Madras, 1907.

E. HARDY.—*Der Buddhismus.* Münster, 1890.

R. PISCHEL.—*Leben und Lehre des Buddha.* Leipzig, 1906.

BIBLIOGRAPHY

There is a very careful list of all European books and articles on Buddhism in

ALBERT J. EDMUNDS.—*Buddhist Bibliography*, in *Journal of the Pali Text Society*, 1903.